At 8:32 AM Pacific Daylight Time, May 18, 1980

Mt. St. Helens Erupted.

Pre-eruption photo of Mt. St. Helens, as viewed from Spirit Lake
Photo © Bob & Suzanne Clemenz

Photo © USGS Photo

Spirit Lake and snow capped Mount St. Helens
Photo © Photri, Inc.

Photo © USGS Photo

Labelled by the U.S. Geological Survey Volcano Hazards Evaluation Team as overdue for an eruption and likely to do so soon, Mount St. Helens began its eruptive process on March 20, 1980. At 3:47 p.m. on that date, an earthquake registering 4.1 on the Richter scale shook the area around the mountain. Thought at first to be centered 18 miles to the northeast, the earthquake did not draw much attention. As the frequency of the tremors in the area increased each day, a reexamination of the first quake showed that its location was centered directly under the volcano. Suddenly, Mount St. Helens was beginning to attract attention. One week to the day from the first sign of activity, Mount St. Helens began puffing steam and ash, clearing her throat, as it were, for what was to come.

This first eruption and the other early eruptions that followed were steam bursts which occurred when heat from the molten magma far beneath the mountain came in

Photo © Dave Olsen

contact with water in the ground. The ash that fell out of these steam plumes was ash that was left deposited in the mountain from the last time the volcano erupted, 123 years before. The early eruptions varied in size and ash content, with some plumes reaching heights of more than a mile above the mountain.

From March 27 until the mountain quieted in late April, the periodic steam eruptions continued, each one expanding the crater until, at the end of April, the crater measured roughly 1000 feet by 1500 feet. At its maximum depth, it measured 800 feet from the higher south summit to the bottom – deep enough to hold an 80-story building and large enough to accomodate nearly 25 football fields. As the growth of the crater continued through April, the frequency of earthquakes around the mountain decreased, although the number of tremors in excess of magnitude 4.0 increased. This fact combined with the fact that the mountain had ceased its steam eruptions and that a bulge on the north face of the mountain was expanding at a rate of 5 feet per day gave little clue as to what would happen next. The answer came on the morning of May 18.

April 27, 1980, by W. Lipman/USGS/CVO/Denver

May 18, 1980

For more than nine hours a vigorous plume of ash erupted, eventually reaching 12 to 15 miles (20-25 kilometers) above sea level. The plume moved eastward at an average speed of 60 miles per hour (95 km/hr), with ash reaching Idaho by noon. By early May 19, the devastating eruption was over. Shown here is a close-up view of the May 18 ash plume.

May 18, 1980, by Donald A. Swanson

On May 18, 1980, at 8:32 a.m. Pacific Daylight Time, a magnitude 5.1 earthquake shook Mount St. Helens. The bulge and surrounding area slid away in a gigantic rockslide and debris avalanche, releasing pressure and triggering a major pumice and ash eruption of the volcano. Thirteen-hundred feet (400 meters) of the peak collapsed or blew outwards. As a result, 24 square miles (62 square kilometers) of valley was filled by a debris avalanche, 250 square miles (650 square kilometers) of recreation, timber and private lands were damaged by a lateral blast, and an estimated 200 million cubic yards (150 million cubic meters) of material was deposited directly by lahars (volcanic mudflows) into the river channels. Fifty-seven people were killed or are still missing.

May 18, 1980, by Austin Post, USGS/CVO/Glaciology Project

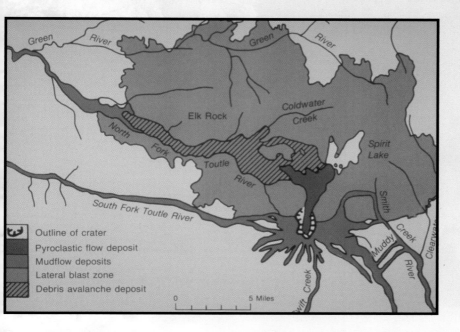

Map of the areas around Mount St. Helens which were affected by the May 18, 1980 eruption. North is to the top.

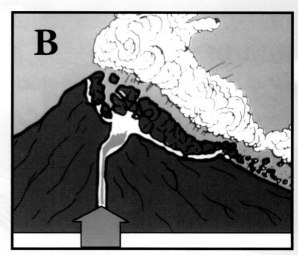

Sequence of the Major Eruption

A)   At 8:30 and again at 8:32 seismographs record earthquakes of magnitude 5.0 or above shaking the mountain. The north face, already weakening and bulging from the pressure of the magma pushing upward, gives way and begins to avalanche down.

B)   Free of the weight of the mountain to contain it, the sublimated gases inside the magma were free to expand; like a shaken champagne bottle with its cork removed, a lateral burst results, focused to the north by the intact west, south and east walls of the crater.

C)   The eruption reaches a peak in a chain reaction. The more magma released, the less the pressure further down in the magma chamber allowing even a greater rush of gas to escape. Pyroclastic flows, a mixture of super heated gases and other volcanic material (ash, cinder, pumice) spill out of the lowered north lip of the crater and descend on Spirit Lake at speeds up to 200 mph.

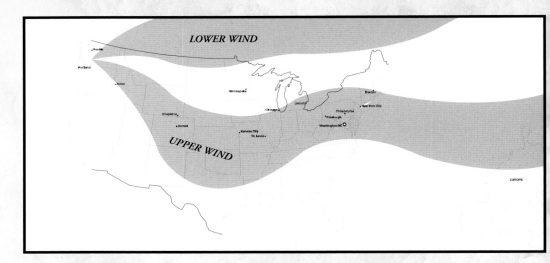

FALLOUT THROUGHOUT THE WORLD

The ash fall formed a thick blanket throughout Eastern Washington, Northern Idaho and Western Montana, varying in depths from one to six inches. The lower part of the plume, carried by lower altitude winds, swept northeastward across Washington and into Canada. Higher altitude winds carried the ash southeast through the U.S. and eventually around the world.

Mud & Ash Flow on the Toutle River

Mounds of ash and mud were deposited below the Mountain during the May 18 eruption. When President Carter inspected the damage caused by the eruption he stated: "It makes the surface of the moon look like a golf course."

Photo © Al Hayward

This downstream view of the North Fork Toutle River valley, northwest of Mount St. Helens, shows part of the nearly 2/3 cubic miles (2.3 cubic kilometers) of debris avalanche that slid from the volcano on May 18. This is enough material to cover Washington, D.C. to a depth of 14 feet (4 meters). The avalanche traveled approximately 15 miles (24 kilometers) downstream at a velocity exceeding 150 miles per hour (240 km/hr). It left behind a hummocky deposit with an average thickness of 150 feet (45 meters) and a maximum thickness of 600 feet (180 meters).

November 30, 1983, by Lyn Topinka, USGS/CVO

Nearly 135 miles (220 kilometers) of river channels surrounding the volcano were affected by the lahars of May 18. A mudline left behind on trees shows depths reached by the mud. A scientist (middle right) gives scale. This view is along the Muddy River, southeast of Mount St. Helens.

October 23, 1980, by Lyn Topinka, USGS/CVO

TOTAL DESTRUCTION IN "BLAST ZONE"

Photo © C.B. Ellis/Smith-Western Co.

Photo © Chuck Adams; Taken November 1997

Meta Lake and Mount St. Helens destruction 11 years later
Photo © D.C. Lowe/FPG

Debris from the blast stretched out for hundreds of miles. Crops within three miles of the mountain were completely destroyed, and Idaho reported eight tons of volcanic ash per acre. Over ten million trees were blown away by volcanic blasts, causing billions of dollars of damage for the logging industry. Downed trees spread across the entire landscape, completely covering the grand hills where forests once stood. The peak of Mount St. Helens that once topped out at 9,680 feet was reduced to a crater that sits at about 8,000 feet high.

Photo © USGS Photo; Taken October 1980

BEFORE & AFTER

Photo Courtesy of Jim Nieland, U.S. Forest Service/Mount St. Helens National Volcanic Monument

May 19, 1982; Photo © Lyn Topinka, USGS/CVO

Johnston Ridge
Photo © Jeffrey L. Torretta

THE CASCADE RANGE - Volcanoes

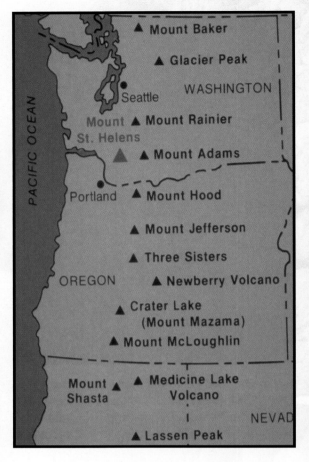

- ▲ Mount Baker
- ▲ Glacier Peak

WASHINGTON

● Seattle

Mount
St. Helens
- ▲ Mount Rainier
- ▲ Mount Adams
- ▲ Mount Hood

● Portland

- ▲ Mount Jefferson
- ▲ Three Sisters

OREGON
- ▲ Newberry Volcano

- ▲ Crater Lake
  (Mount Mazama)
- ▲ Mount McLoughlin

PACIFIC OCEAN

Mount
Shasta
- ▲ Medicine Lake
  Volcano

NEVAD

- ▲ Lassen Peak

MSH erupts in 1980 with Mt. Rainier in background
Photo Courtesy of North Cascades National Park

Mt. Adams is visible to the east of MSH
Photo © Chuck Adams

Mt. Rainier rises in background with forest devastation in foreground

Photo © Jon Gnass/Gnass Photo Images

Mt. Hood is visible to the south of MSH devastation

Photo © Christian Heeb/Gnass Photo Images

Mount St. Helens has continued to erupt throughout the ensuing years. An explosive eruption on March 19, 1982, sent pumice and ash 9 miles (14 kilometers) into the air, and resulted in a lahar (the dark deposit on the snow) flowing from the crater into the North Fork Toutle River valley. Part of the lahar entered Spirit Lake (lower left corner) but most of the flow went west down the Toutle River, eventually reaching the Cowlitz River, 50 miles (80 kilometers) downstream.

March 21, 1982,
by Thomas J. Casadevall,
USGS/CVO

During the May 18, 1980 eruption, at least 17 separate pyroclastic flows descended the flanks of Mount St. Helens. Pyroclastic flows typically move at speeds of over 60 miles per hour (100 km/hr) and reach temperatures of over 800 Degrees Fahrenheit (400 degrees Celsius). Photographed here, a pyroclastic flow stretches from Mount St. Helens' crater to the valley floor below, during an eruption August 7, 1980.

August 7, 1980, by Peter W. Lipman,
USGS/CVO

Photo © Smith-Western, Inc.

Plumes of steam, gas, and ash often occur at Mount St. Helens. On clear days they can be seen from Portland, Oregon, 50 miles (81 kilometers) to the south. The plume photographed here rose nearly 3000 feet (1000 meters) above the volcano's rim. The view is from Harry's Ridge, five miles (8 kilometers) north of the mountain.

May 19, 1982, by Lyn Topinka,
USGS/CVO

Five more explosive eruptions of Mount St. Helens occurred during 1980, including this spectacular event of July 22. This eruption sent pumice and ash 6 to 11 miles (10-18 kilometers) into the air, and was visible in Seattle, Washington, 100 miles (160 kilometers) to the north. The view here (above) is from the south of the mountain.

July 22, 1980, by Michael P. Doukas,
USGS/CVO

LAVA DOME

Aerial view of the lava dome inside the crater
Photo © C.B. Ellis

Since December 1980, eruptions of Mount St. Helens have added material to dacitic lava dome with the crater, as seen here in this 1984 view from the north. This dome was not the first dome to grow in the crater. In June and August 1980, two domes formed, only to be blasted away by the explosive events of July 22 and October 16.

September 13, 1984,
by Lyn Topinka,
USGS/CVO

A new dome started growing on October 18, 1980. This October dome was 112 feet (34 meters) high and 985 feet (300 meters) wide, making it taller than a nine-story building and wider than the length of three football fields. This aerial view is from the north.

October 24, 1980,
by Terry A. Leighley,
USGS/CVO/Sandia Labs

Two U.S. Geological Survey geologists (one in orange, middle right, near base of dome) are dwarfed by the dome. The geologists stand on snow muddied from recent ashfall. By 1990, the dome had replaced only three percent of the volume removed by the May 18, 1980 eruption. If this rate of growth continues it would take over 200 years to rebuild Mount St. Helens to its pre-1980 size.

May 26, 1983,
by Lyn Topinka,
USGS/CVO

The most recent dome-building eruption of Mount St. Helens occurred in October 1986. A new lobe was extruded, increasing the dome's height to 925 feet (282 meters), making it taller than a 77-story building. In this 30-minute, moon-lit exposure, hot rock from the new lobe is seen glowing on top of the dome. The view is from Harrys Ridge, five miles (8 kilometers) north of the volcano.

October 22, 1986, at 8:50 p.m.,
by Lyn Topinka,
USGS/CVO

LIFE RETURNS TO A DEVASTATED AREA

Wildflowers abound in once devastated areas
Photo © Chuck Adams; Taken July 1998

Wildflowers & fir trees flourish amid the once desolate blast area.
Photo © John Elk III

Photo © Gary Greene

Coldwater Creek, 1999
Photo © J. Poehlman

The "New" Spirit Lake
Photo © Bob & Suzanne Clemenz; Taken 1992

Highway 504 Bridge
Photo © John Elk III

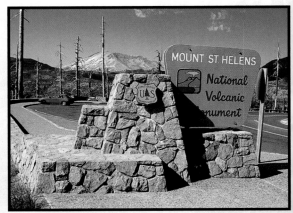

Photo © Jack Olson

Johnston Ridge & Pumice Plain
Photo © Jeffrey L. Torretta

In 1982, President Reagan and Congress created the 110,000-acre National Volcanic Monument for research, recreation and education. Inside the monument, the land has been left undisturbed to develop naturally and recover from the volcanic disturbance. The fallen north face of Mount St. Helens has reshaped the "New" Spirit Lake by lifting it about 200 feet higher and pushing its south beach in. Downed logs still float across the lake's surface, occasionally sinking to the bottom and rooting into the floor, creating a sunken forest below the waters.

MOUNT ST. HELENS NATIONAL VOLCANIC MONUMENT

Mount St. Helens Visitor Center, Silver Lake
Photo © John Elk III

North Fork Ridge Visitor Center
Photo © John Elk III

Windy Ridge Viewpoint
Photo © Bob & Suzanne Clemenz

Johnston Ridge Observatory
Photo © Chuck Adams

Coldwater Lake from Coldwater Ridge Visitor Center
Photo © Gary Greene

Coldwater Ridge Visitor Center
Photo © John Elk III

MOUNT ST. HELENS NATIONAL VOLCANIC MONUMENT

From Windy Ridge
Photo © John Elk III

The modern face of Mount St. Helens is quite different from the images we are familiar with: the explosive angry volcano, emanating thick dark smoke. Today, the mountain is serene, a crater rests where a peak once stood, and the area around it is cleared of its forests. It is a calm reminder of what happened many years ago, May 18, 1980.

Photo © Gary Greene

Photo © Chuck Adams

Winter View from South Side
Photo © Jon Gnass/Gnass Photo Images